Volume
19

Komi Can't Communicate

Tomohito Oda

19 Contents

Komi Can't Communicate

The phrase *communication disorder*...

... describes a range of symp-toms...
...related to a difficulty interacting with others.
For example ...

...a person with a communication disorder...
...!
VISIT THE LIBRARY!
BOOKS ARE HERE!
FWIP
...may forget how to interact...
VISIT THE LIBRARY!
...when seeing a friend again for the first time in a while.
VISIT THE LIBRARY!
TREMMMBLE

Communication 247: Out of Sync

Komi's tor-ment
That's what happened.

"I should have said hello, but Agari didn't make eye contact. Maybe she just didn't notice me, but now I don't know what to do."
THAT JUST HAPPENS SOMETIMES!
OH, I SEE...
I TOTALLY KNOW THAT FEELING !!

"I'm afraid she hates me."
NO, I DOUBT THAT.
!

"What would you two do?"
What would you two do?

I UNDERSTAND HOW YOU FEEL, BUT...
...I'D PROBABLY JUST SAY HELLO.

WHEN I SEE FRIENDS, I GET ALL HYPER AND I CAN'T KEEP MY MOUTH SHUT!
PWAAAH

GLOOOOOOM
BUT THEN IF THEY ACT LOW-KEY...
...IT'S AWKWARD AND I GET BUMMED.
!!

"How about you, Ase?"
How about you, Ase?
!

I WOULDN'T SAY ANYTHING. I DON'T HAVE ANYTHING INTERESTING TO SAY...
...AND MAYBE THEY FORGOT ME.

NO WAY, SHIBBY! IF YOU'RE EVER IN MY NEIGHBORHOOD AND YOU SEE ME COLLAPSED ON THE GROUND IN WORN-OUT SWEATS CLUTCHING A CONVENIENCE STORE BAG, YOU GOTTA SAY HI! IT'D PERK ME UP!
OKAY?!
HUH? UM... OKAY.
WHAT A SPECIFIC HYPO-THETICAL SITUATION!
T

I THINK WE ALL KNOW WHAT NAJIMI WOULD DO.
YIPPEEE
YAAAY
YAHOOO
...

Agari's tor-ment

SHE DIDN'T REMEMBER YOU.
WHAM
GACK
DON'T SAY THAT, DAD!
...!
A

NITA DINER
THAT'S NOT TRUE! KOMI ATE HERE WITH YOU, DIDN'T SHE?
WHEN DID YOU LAST SPEAK?
UM... THREE MONTHS AGO, AT A FESTIVAL.
*See communication 61.

THREE WHOLE MONTHS? AT THE SAME SCHOOL?!
WHOA, THAT'S BAD...
?!
GAGAAACK
A

NO WORRIES! YOU CAN START OVER FROM SCRATCH!
GWUP
Not very encour-aging
...

IT'S ALL RIGHT... I BARELY MAKE AN IMPRESSION ANYWAY...
BWA BWA
GULP GULP
Stress eating

TRY TALKING TO HER AGAIN.
DEEP-FRIED CHICKEN MEAL 7.50
CHICKEN CUTLET 8.00
GRILLED FISH MEAL 6.50
PORK CUTLET BOWL 7.50
I BET SHE *WANTS* YOU TO!

IF I GUD DO DAT, DERE'D BE NO PROB-BEM!!
LICK LICK
SLAMMM
IS SHE DRUNK? ON *WATER?!*
LOOKS LIKE IT...

The next day
!
T-TODAY, I ABSOLUTELY MUST...
...SAY "GOOD MORNING!"
HUFF
HUFF
BABMP
BABMP
BABMP
BABMP
G...
GWOOO
?!

...
FWIP
GACK
!!
IT HAPPENED AGAIN!!

Agari's tor- ment
GLOOM
I KNEW IT! SHE HATES ME!! DID I DO SOMETHING WRONG?!

Flash- back
TRY ASKING YOUR SCHOOL- MATES.
?
NO... GORIMI IS TOO SCARY...

SIGH...
AND I BARELY HAVE ANY FRIENDS ...

!

BUT NAKANAKA WAS IN MY GROUP ON THE SCHOOL TRIP, AND WE BORROW EACH OTHER'S BOOKS...
...SO WE'RE FRIENDS, RIGHT?! I'LL ASK HER ABOUT KOMI!!
Unsettled by Agari zooming in
DO I EVEN EXIST?

DOOM
DOOM
Komi's tor-ment
WHAT'S WRONG?
SHE SAID IT HAPPENED AGAIN AND IT WAS OBVIOUS.

Takara-zuka's advice
HOW TO APPROACH A FRIEND AFTER TIME APART?
!
NOD NOD
TRY *THIS* ON HER...

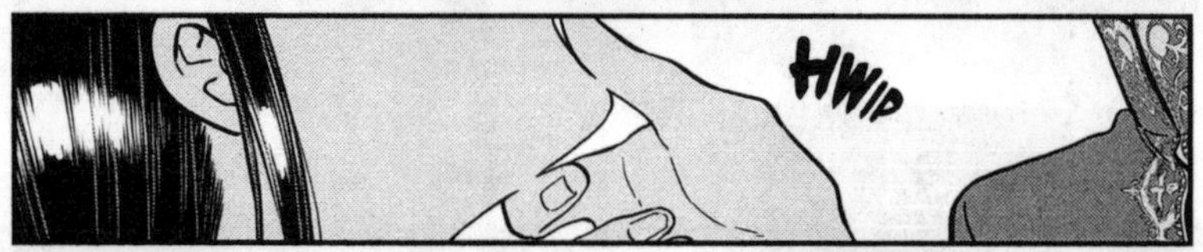
HWIP

"I MISTOOK YOU FOR A FLOWER, MADEMOI-SELLE."
...SELLE... SELLE...
Echo
?!

Toro's advice
...
HEH...
TRMBL TRMBL
"Am I bug-ging her?"

HM?
AHH!
CHAK
STAGGER
!

"OOPS! I TRIPPED!"
Umph!
Huff
Umph!
HOW ABOUT THAT?
?!

Isagi's advice
I WOULD IGNORE HER.
?!

That after-noon
SUNSET ALREADY?! THE DAYS SURE ARE GETTING SHORTER!
YEAH.
!
I'VE GOT TO TALK TO HER THIS TIME!
RIGHT HERE! RIGHT NOW!

SW IP
IT'S NO USE... WE'LL NEVER SPEAK AGAIN.
I GUESS ...
...WE AREN'T FRIENDS ANYMORE.
BUT I WANTED ...
...TO SAY GOOD MORNING.

...
G...
GOOD...
...MORNING.
!!

YEAH!

GOOD MORNING TO YOU TOO!

Communication 247 — The End

Komi Can't Communicate

Communication 248: Ear Takeaway

WHAT SONG IS THAT?
?
OH, THE ONE I'VE BEEN HUMMING?

I'VE HAD A BAD CASE OF EAR TAKEAWAY SINCE YESTERDAY!
IT'S A COMMERCIAL, BUT I'M NOT SURE ABOUT THE LYRICS!
...

YOU KNOW HOW IT IS!
SOMETIMES BACKGROUND MUSIC ...
...OR A SONG SOMEONE IS SINGING WILL GIVE YOU EAR TAKEAWAY!
...

ALL DAY LONG, I'VE HAD EAR TAKEAWAY!
AH HA HA HA HA
...

WHAT DO YOU MEAN BY EAR TAKEAWAY?
HUH?

DON'T PEOPLE SAY THAT WHEN A SONG GETS STUCK IN THEIR HEAD?
LIKE, "I'VE GOT EAR TAKE-AWAY!"
HUH?
HUH?

HWUP
SH-SHOKO! "EAR TAKEAWAY" IS A PHRASE, RIGHT?!

...
Has never heard that
!!

I'M NOT FINDING IT ONLINE.
SERI-OUSLY ?!

SO ONLY PEOPLE AROUND ME SAY THAT?
HEY! YOU GUYS SHOULD START!
UM, NO THANK YOU...

Fifth period
Doot-doot-doot!
La-di-da-da!

Sixth period
Doot-deet-doot! Tra-laaa!

Doot-doot-doot! La-di-da-da!
Faintly swaying to the rhythm
Doot-deet-doot! Tra-laaa!
Doot-deet-doot! Tra-laaa!
KOMI GOT EAR TAKE-AWAY!!
T

Doot-doot-doot...
La-di-da-da.
KATAI TOO?!

*Doot-doot-doot...
...la-di-da-da...
Doot-deet-doot! Tra-laaa!
IT'S SPREADING!

I'M HOME!
Good morning!
YAY
YAY
CHATTER
CHATTER

REE-REE-RE-FRESHING! ♪

YOU GOT **EAR TAKE-AWAY!!**

Communication 248 — The End

Komi Can't Communicate

PWAAAAAH

HEY, EVERY-BODY! LET'S ALL SKIP!

?!

Communication 249: Skipping

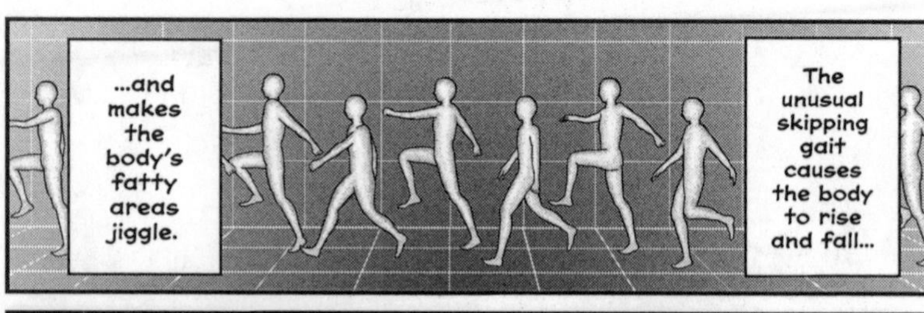
The unusual skipping gait causes the body to rise and fall...
...and makes the body's fatty areas jiggle.

That's right. Ren Yamai is imagining Komi skipping, complete with heaving chest and brief flashes of underwear.
*Yamai's fantasy goes here.

Yamai is surprised at her own presence of mind in asking everyone and not just Komi.
KO-MI!
KOMI!! LET'S PLAY TWISTER! I BROUGHT IT ALL THE WAY FROM VENEZIA!
TWISTER
Of course, it's merely a ruse to avoid arousing Komi's suspicion...
...but she usually fails to do this.

Armed with a plan, feeling firm of will and sufficiently stealthy ...
...she has a totally different aura today!
...

I haven't skipped in ages! Like two weeks!
THAT'S PRETTY RECENT.
Komi! Have you ever skipped? Give it a try!
!

Amazed at her good fortune...
...Yamai coolly prepares her gear.
8K camera
?!

Komi skipping
HIP
HOP
Ah ha ha! Talk about clunky!
YEAH, BUT SHE'S DOING IT!

HUAM MMM MMM FFF!!
SMAKKOOM
?!

THAT WAS CLOSE! SHE ALMOST PURIFIED ME!
HFF
HFF
...
BUT I CAN'T RELEASE ALL MY IMPURITIES UNTIL I SEE HER UNDIES!

I'VE NEVER SKIPPED BE-FORE.
IS IT THAT UNUSUAL?
YOU'RE 17 AND YOU'VE NEVER SKIPPED?!
WELL, HERE'S YOUR CHANCE TO PRACTICE! YOU TOO, KATAI! THIS'LL BE *HILARIOUS!*
!

Katai skip-ping
HWUP
HWUP
Skipping Note #1
Smile as you skip.
THIS IS TERRI-FYING!

Rumiko skip-ping
HOO!
FLOINK
HAA!
FLOINK
?!

WA HA HA HA HA HA!
UM... WHAT WAS THAT?!
?!
?!
HUH? WHAT DO YOU MEAN?!
WA HA HA HA HA HA!

UM... SHOW HER HOW IT'S DONE, KOMI.
WHEEEEEEW
!!

Komi skip-ping
FLOINK
FLOINK
?!
MANBAGI'S PROBLEM IS SPREADING!!
?!

FLOINK
FLOINK
FLOINK
ARGH!! KOMI IS SKIPPING LIKE A NEWBORN FAWN!
THAT GYARU IS ALWAYS HOGGING KOMI TO HERSELF, AND NOW SHE WON'T LET ME SEE HER UNDERPANTS!

HUH?! THIS ISN'T RIGHT?!
FLOINK
FLOINK
I'M SO CONFUSED! WHAT DO I DO?!

YOU'RE HOPE-LESS.
!!

RAISE YOUR KNEES HIGHER AND...
...HOP ON ONE FOOT, THEN THEN THE OTHER.
!
OKAY, I'LL TRY THAT.
TH-THANKS ...
...UM, YAMAI.

Communication 249 — The End

Had
a bad
feeling,
so she
wore
shorts

Komi Can't Communicate

Komi Can't Communicate

Communication 250: Fantasies, Part 3

Who would you date? -Ase-
DIDN'T SOMETHING LIKE THIS HAPPEN BEFORE?
G
*See Vol. 6, communication 75

KAPLONK
THANKS FOR WAITING. DID YOU GET COLD?
NO, I JUST GOT OUT NOW.
OH, GOOD!

THE NIGHT AIR FEELS GOOD.
YEAH, IT DOES!

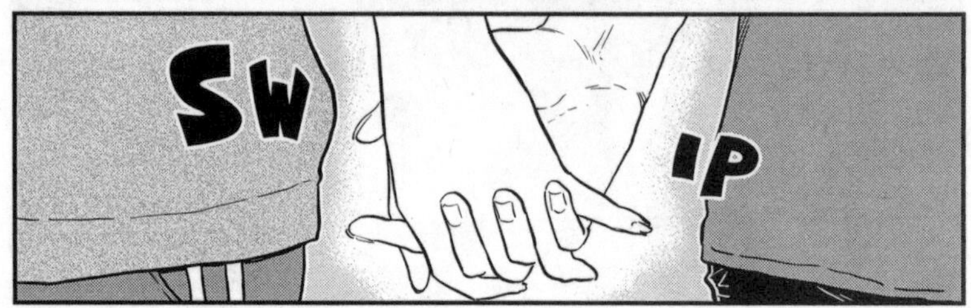
SW
IP

...

I JUST TOOK A BATH, BUT...
...I'M ALREADY SWEATING.

NONE-THELESS, SHE DOES NOT LET GO.
A = Shigeo Chiarai
NICE FANTASY ...
YOU CAPTURED ASE'S ESSENCE.
THE FANTASIES GIVE EVERYONE AWAY!
*This scene was pure fantasy.
Any relation to real persons or events is coincidental.

Who would you date?
-Fushima-
TAK TAK TAK
TAK TAK
SKRK SKRK
TAK TAK
FUSHIMA ?!

WHEW! I FINALLY FINISHED!!
GOOD JOB! JUST IN TIME FOR THE PRINTER DEADLINE!
YEAH! THANKS FOR YOUR HELP!

IS YOUR COSTUME READY FOR THE SALES FLOOR?
YEAH! A FRIEND ONLINE MADE IT!
I'LL GO PUT IT ON!

TADA! I'M RAMURA FROM USHIEN!!
ISN'T IT HIGH QUALITY ?!

...
YOU'VE GOT PRETTY SKIN, FUSHI.

NO...
LOOK AT THE COSTUME!

WITH BETTER HAIR, SHE TOTALLY CHANGES!
B = Taisei Sonoda
B
SERI-OUSLY?
I NEVER KNEW SHE HAD SUCH POTENTIAL ...
D
I'LL LOOK AT HER IN A NEW LIGHT NOW.
G
THAT'S FOR SURE!
G
*This scene was pure fantasy.
Any relation to real persons or events is coincidental.

Who would you date?
-Sato-
SATO...

...WILL YOU GO OUT WITH ME?
BOW
SURE!
REALLY ?!

Three years later...
THREE YEARS LATER?!

CLINK
YOU AGREED TO GO OUT WITH ME RIGHT AWAY, BUT...
...AM I REALLY GOOD ENOUGH?

YOU SILLY!
I WOULDN'T SAY "SURE" TO JUST ANYONE!

IN THAT MOMENT, I VOWED TO DEDICATE MY LIFE TO HER.
C = Mono Shinobino
I THINK I MIGHT CRY...
THIS WAS A QUALITY FANTASY.
I LIKED IT TOO.
*This scene was pure fantasy. Any relation to real persons or events is coincidental.

Who would you date?
-Isagi-
ISAGI!
MY GIRLFRIEND IS THE STUDENT COUNCIL PRESIDENT.
SHALL WE RIDE THE TRAIN HOME TOGETHER?
SMOOTH
WHO IS THAT?!
G
NO. I'M BUSY.
I UNDERSTAND. YOU HAVE STUDENT COUNCIL WORK.
I LOVE HER DEDICATION AS A REPRESENTATIVE OF THE STUDENT BODY...
...
...BUT SOMETIMES I GET LONELY.
BAM

FSHHHH
!
WHAT ABOUT YOUR WORK?
I FINISHED IT.
HUH?

HUFF
HUFF
IS THAT A PROB-LEM?

CLAP
YOU'VE PORTRAYED HER TO PERFECTION.
D = Son Totoi
CLAP
BRAVO!
CLAP
APPLAUSE ?!
*This scene was pure fantasy. Any relation to real persons or events is coincidental.

Who would you date?
-Manbagi-
THAT LOOKS FUN! LET'S DO IT!
ONE DAY, I WAS WITH MY GIRLFRIEND AT A TRAMPOLINE PARK.

THE NAME'S SHUKIO OHAI.
HOW TOMBOYISH OF YOU! ☆
A MALE VERSION OF OHAI?!
G

AH HA HA! COME JOIN ME, SHUKIO!
PYOING
PYOING

BYOING
JIGGLE
BYOING
JIGGLE

BYOMMMP
KYAH!
!

AH HA HA!
MY LEGS ARE GETTING SHAKY!

E = Shuki Ohai
MY THEMES WERE STILLNESS AND MOVEMENT.
NICE BOOB ACTION!
A
B
C
D
F
B
G
THEY'RE INCORRIGIBLE...
*This scene was pure fantasy. Any relation to real persons or events is coincidental.

UM... UM...
...W-WILL YOU...
HUH?
...GO OUT WITH ME?
THAT'S ME!!

IS ANYTHING...

...WRONG WITH THAT?

IF THAT CON-CLUDES THE MINOR EPISODES...
IT'S NOW TIME FOR MONTHLY KOMI.
"MONTHLY KOMI"?!
G

LAST TIME, A SERIES OF UNUSUAL EVENTS LED TO US TRAVELING BACK IN TIME TO THE CRETACEOUS PERIOD, WHERE WE DEFEATED A DINOSAUR, THEN BACK TO THE PRESENT TO SHARE A MEAL.
TIME TRAVEL? TO THE CRETACEOUS PERIOD?!
G

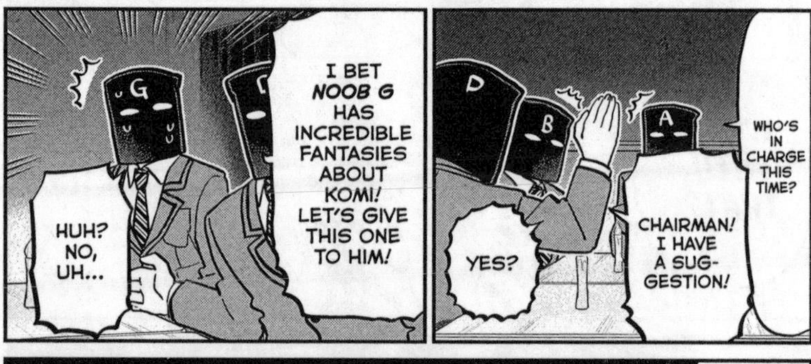
WHO'S IN CHARGE THIS TIME?
CHAIRMAN! I HAVE A SUG-GESTION!
YES?
I BET NOOB G HAS INCREDIBLE FANTASIES ABOUT KOMI! LET'S GIVE THIS ONE TO HIM!
HUH? NO, UH...

OH? THEN GIVE IT A TRY.
CAN YOU OUT-FANTASIZE US?
HEH HEH HEH...
?!
G

Who would you date?
-Komi-
THERE'S AN EMPTY BENCH, KOMI.
!
SHALL WE EAT HAVE A SNACK THERE?
NOD NOD
!!

THE SAKURA TREES SURE ARE PRETTY!

Al-
ready
two
gone.

WERE YOU HUNGRY ?

BLUSHHH
...
!

G
H-HOW WAS THAT?
N-N-N-NOT BAD AT ALL!!
A
NO WAY! WE STRUGGLE WITH KOMI, BUT IT WAS EASY FOR HIM!!
B
HE'S A KOMI-FANTASIST EXTRAOR-DINAIRE!!
...
C
HOW DID HE DO THAT?!
*This scene was pure fantasy.
Any relation to real persons or events is coincidental.

TADANO, THANK YOU FOR ATTENDING THIS OFF-SITE MEETING OF *THE RIVERSIDE MAGAZINE HUNTERS CLUB.*
HUH? NO PROBLEM. WAIT... HUH?

YOUR KOMI FANTASY WAS IMPRESSIVE. DO YOU FANTASIZE ABOUT HER OFTEN?
N-NO, OF COURSE NOT!!
YOU'RE SO MODEST. HA HA!
TEE HEE HEE!
AH HA HA!
I DON'T DO THAT!!

IT'S DIFFICULT FINDING THE PERFECT KOMI FANTASY...
...SO I HOPE YOU'LL ATTEND AGAIN SOME-TIME.
HUH?

Communication 250 — The End

Komi Can't Communicate

HEY, KOMI...
...HAVE YOU MADE ANY NEW FRIENDS RECENTLY?

...!
FWIPFWIP
...
*Komi's Book of Friends lists all her friends.
KOMI'S BOOK OF FRIENDS

Lemme see that!
SNATCH
!!
KOMI'S BOOK OF FRIENDS

Only eight new friends this year?
Are you even trying?
!!!
KIYOKO ISAGI

Komi Can't Communicate

Communication 251: Singles Meetup?

PHYSICS
?!

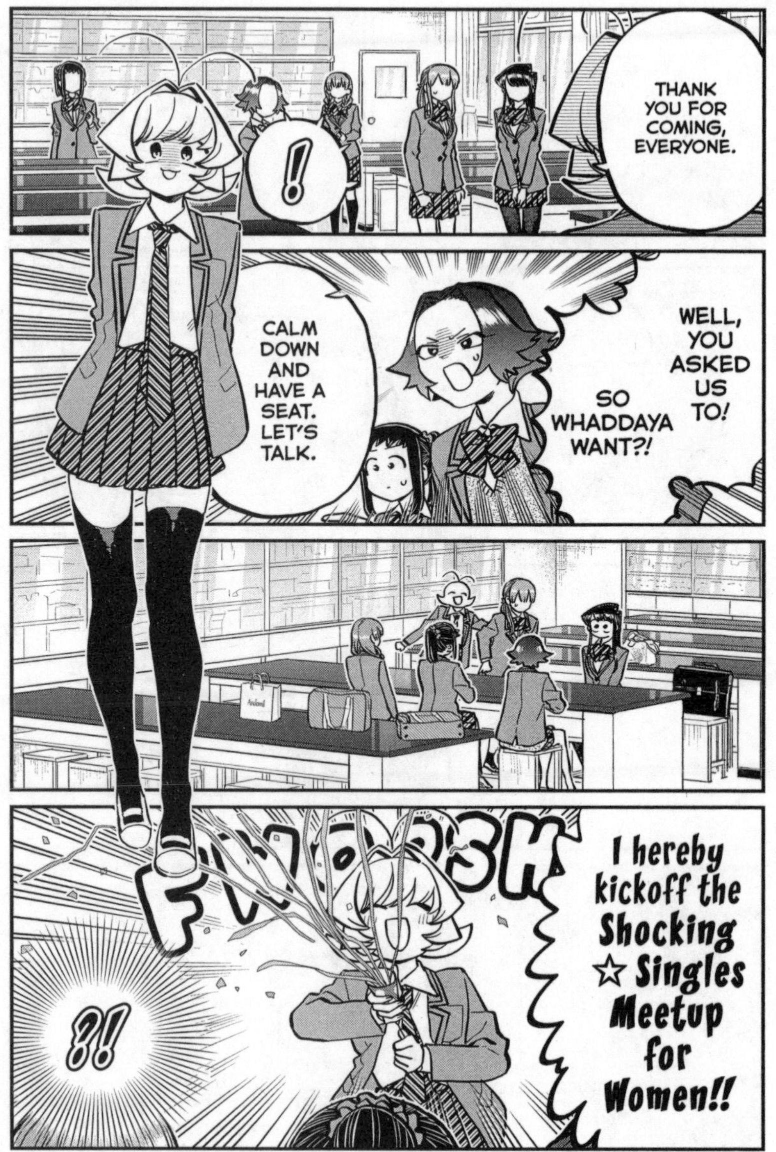
THANK YOU FOR COMING, EVERYONE.
!
WELL, YOU ASKED US TO!
SO WHADDAYA WANT?!
CALM DOWN AND HAVE A SEAT. LET'S TALK.
I hereby kickoff the Shocking ☆ Singles Meetup for Women!!
FWOOSH
?!

Start by intro-ducing your-selves!
HOLD ON A SECOND!! WHAT THE HELL?! SHOULDN'T THERE BE BOYS HERE TOO?!
Not this time! You seem enthusiastic, Anchi! So you go first!
HUNH ?!

~ ~ ~

I'M ARISA ANCHI ...
...FROM CLASS 2-3.

HUH? THAT'S ALL? TELL US SOMETHING YOU LIKE!
B-o-o-o-ring!
HUNH ?!

WELL, I DON'T REALLY...
...LIKE ANY-THING.
SO THAT'S ALL.

...
GLANCE

HMPH
?

OKAY, THANKS.
NEXT! GOING CLOCK-WISE!
!

M-ME? YEAH, ME... OR IS IT?
WHICH WAY DO CLOCKS GO?! UM, UM...

WELL, GET TO IT! WHY SO SLOW?!
First meeting
EEP! S-SORRY!
Anchi is antagonistic.

I'M SAKI TSUZURAFUJI FROM, UM, CLASS 2-2.
AND I LIKE, UH...

W-WHAT DO I LIKE? M-MAYBE DORAYAKI PANCAKES?!
BUT THAT'S SO JAPANESE! THEY MIGHT TEASE ME!
Copyright
THAT WOULD BREAK THE ICE, BUT, UM...
Impression

I LIKE, UM, YOU-KNOW-WHAT!
HUH?
WE DO?
WE KNOW...
...WHAT?
?
Tsuzurafuji overthinks things.

Kogoen speaks softly.

I'm everybody's favorite, Najimi! I like fatty tuna and hate studying!
Sign-Aries! Blood type-AB!
Here, lemme show you some-thing funny!

PHBBBBT! THBBT! THBBT! FBRRRRT!
RRRRING!!!
HM?

HELLO?
UH-HUH!
MM?
SERI-OUSLY?
YEAH!
I'LL BE RIGHT THERE!
NO PROB-LEM!

WHAT?! A HAMMER-HEAD SHARK?!
CHAK
?!

NAJIMI LEFT US!
SH- SHOULD WE END THE MEETING?
BUT WE CAME FOR A REASON, RIGHT?
AND YET...

...
...

WELL ...
...NOW WHAT?
!
!
!
!

...
WHADDAYA MEAN, "NOW WHAT"?!

...
ISN'T EVERYONE GOING TO LEAVE?

UM...
WELL THEN...
...SHALL WE...
...CON-TINUE?

YES, LET'S.
I GUESS SO...
YEAH.
T
THEY WANT TO STAY?!

I'M, UM... HITOMI TADANO ...
...FROM CLASS 2-1.
AND I LIKE... MANGA? I GUESS?

PLEASED TO MEET YOU!
BOW

WHAT AM I DOING?!
Wants to die

WHY AM I DRESSED LIKE A GIRL?!
Doesn't anyone notice?
It's Najimi's fault.
Don't worry! Trust in Naji!

STAAARE
Now it's her turn.
!

H-HMPH

H... HMPH
TWICE?!

CHAK

...
...

W-WHAT'S GOING ON?! SHOULD I SAY SOME-THING?!
W-WHY IS EVERYONE JUST WAITING ?!
IS THIS A PERFOR-MANCE? DO WE GOTTA BE QUIET?!

I...

I'M...
...SH
...
...SHOKO...
...
KOMI.
...!
...
FUMP
...

CLAP
CLAP CLAP
CLAP
!

CLAP CLAP CLAP CLAP CLAP CLAP CLAP CLAP
HUH? WHAT? THAT'S ALL?
SH-SHE'S DONE? AND NOW WE CLAP?
WOW! KOMI'S SO PRETTY!

WHAT THE HELL?!

YOU DIDN'T SAY WHAT YOU LIKE! OR YOUR CLASS!
YOU BARELY EVEN SAID YOUR NAME!
!

BESIDES, YOU'RE DISGUSTINGLY POPULAR, SO WHY ARE YOU EVEN HERE?
I BET YOU LOOK DOWN ON US.

BUT YOU PRETEND TO BE AWKWARD AND CUTE...
...TO WIN PEOPLE OVER.
WELL, YOUR TECHNIQUE IS OBVIOUS.

AND THE REST OF YOU!
YOU DIDN'T CLAP FOR ANYONE ELSE...
...SO WHY CLAP FOR HER?
WHY DOES KOMI GET SPECIAL TREAT-MENT?

BESIDES ...

Communication 251 — The End

Komi Can't Communicate

Communication 252 — Singles Meetup?, Part 2

AH HA... HA...
...
...

HOW DID KOMI REACT?

SPARKLE
WHEW... SHE'S FINE.

Unable to fight back, she's almost in tears.
TREMMMMBLE
OR MAYBE NOT.

MAYBE THIS CAN GIVE US CONVERSATION TOPICS!

WHAT'S ONE OF YOUR HOBBIES?

I BET NAJIMI LEFT IT HERE.

SHALL WE GIVE IT A TRY?

I GUESS, UM...
...I'LL ...
I'LL GO FIRST!

ROLL ROLL ROLL ROLL
DO A TRICK

ROLL
DO A FUNNY IMPRESSION
DARN YOU, NAJIMI!!
That's not a topic!!

OKAY ...
...UM ...
...I'LL DO AN IMPRES-SION.
AHEM ...

...
...

Impression
"ONE TRUTH PREVAILS!"
Impression
"I'M TEEN DETECTIVE JIMMY KUDO."

CLAP CLAP CLAP CLAP CLAP CLAP
DARN YOU, NAJIMI!!!
Doesn't watch TV
?
HMPH HMPH
Excited to see this new side of him

DON'T OVER-THINK IT!
OR... MAYBE NOT SO MUCH?
WAS THAT GOOD? OR NOT? YEAH, IT WAS! FOR A GIRL!

I'LL ROLL NEXT.
UM... GO RIGHT AHEAD?
?

ROLL ROLL
WHAT'S A PERSONAL STRENGTH?
!

HMM... MAYBE MY STRENGTH IS MY BRAVERY.
FOR EXAMPLE, I'M NOT AFRAID OF ANYTHING ON THAT DIE.
SO I'LL DO AN IMPRESSION.
I CAN'T HEAR WHAT SHE'S SAYING!

"SOKECHUUU! SOKE!"
"S-O-O-O-K-E-E-E-CH-U-U-U!"
TEE HEE! HOW WAS IT?
IT WAS REALLY... YEAH!!
A vague response

AM I NEXT?! I'M SO NERVOUS!! WHAT IF I HAVE TO DO AN IMPRESSION?!
THAT TADANO GIRL'S IMPRESSION WAS GOOD! AND IT'S IMPOSSIBLE TO BACK OUT!! YIIIKES!

ROLL
ROLL
DO A TRICK
PHEW!

I CAN MOVE MY EYES OPPOSITE DIRECTIONS.
I WAS SO RELIEVED, I I DIDN'T HESITATE! BUT IS IT TOO BORING?!

WOW... I'M IMPRESSED.
OH, SOME PEOPLE CAN DO THAT?
CHATTER
CHATTER
!!
...
I DID IT! AND THEY LIKE IT!!
OR MAYBE THEY'RE CREEPED OUT?!

...
UM...

...
...

ROLL ROLL
WHAT'S ONE OF YOUR HOBBIES?
WHEW... SHE'S JOINING!

NAH, I PASS.
!!

H-HOW ABOUT YOU, KOMI?
!
WHAT IF IT'S AN IMPRESSION?

ROLL
ROLL
TALK ABOUT HAVING NO FRIENDS
?!
THAT'S A HARSH ONE!!

SKRK SKRK
SKRK

SWUP
Just a second.
!

SKRK
SKRK
SKRK
SKRK
SKRK
SKRK
SKRK
RUB
RUB
RUB
RUB
RUB
!
SKRK
SKRK
SKRK
SKRK
SKRK
SKRK
SKRK
SKRK
SKRK
SKRK
SKRK
I didn't have any friends until high school.
SWUP
!

Because I was afraid of talking in front of people and I couldn't overcome my shyness.
FWIP

"So in junior high..."
"...I asked my cat plushy Noir..."
"...how to communicate better."
*See vol. 1, communication 4.

...!
So in junior high, I asked my cat plushy Noir how to communicate better.
Wants to die
T
SHE HAD A SECRET HISTORY!

HUNH?
ARE YOU STILL PUTTING ON THIS ACT?
THAT NOTEBOOK IS SO AFFECTED.
I DON'T KNOW WHAT YOU'RE AFTER, BUT...
...IF YOU WANT US TO FAWN OVER YOU...
...THEN I'M—
But then I made lots of friends in high school.
...!
"Each one is unique. They're fun and kind and surprising."
"And I'm sure any new friends I make..."
"...will be fun and kind and surprising in their own way."

So I want to make 100 friends.

I want to be friends with everyone here.

I D-DO TOO, BUT...
...AM I...
...G-GOOD ENOUGH ?

I'M NOT PRETTY OR SMART ...
...AND I OVERTHINK EVERY-THING...
...AND I'M SUPER AWK-WARD.
I CAN MOVE MY EYES WEIRD...
...BUT IS THAT ENOUGH ?

UM...
...I...
...WANT TO BE FRIENDS TOO.
Andomil

with everyone here.

SWUP

Andomil

MY HOBBY...

...IS DRAGGING POPULAR POSTS AND FLAMING UNPOPULAR POSTS...
...ON SOCIAL NETWORKS LIKE TOGYATHER.

I'M GOOD AT SPOTTING FAULTS.
AND I LIKE POINTING THEM OUT...
...SO I LOST ALL MY FRIENDS.

BUT I CAN'T STOP.

YOU'RE ALL PRE-TENDING TO BE NICE...
...BUT YOU DON'T KNOW A THING ABOUT ME.
WHO'D WANT TO BE FRIENDS WITH SOMEONE SO ROTTEN?

HMMP
I want to be friends with everyone here.
...?!

ONLY AN AMATEUR SAYS WHO HE'S IMPERSONATING!
YOUR IMPRESSION SUCKED!!
?!
YOU TALK TOO SOFT! USE A MEGAPHONE!!
AND YOUR EYES ARE CLOSED! CAN YOU EVEN SEE?!
!
YOUR FACE IS PLAIN! AND SO IS THAT EYE TRICK!
AND YOU MAKE FUNNY FACES WHEN YOU'RE THINKING!
?!
YOU, WITH COMMUNICATION DISORDER!
YOUR CAT PLUSHY'S NAME IS IMMATURE!
!!

Communication 252 — The End

Komi Can't Communicate

Communication 253: Singles Meetup?, Part 3

ACTUALLY, I'M OKAY WITH INSULTS TO MY FACE.
Andomil
UMPH
WHY?! ARE YOU A MAS-OCHIST?!

ME TOO. I TAKE IT AS GOOD-NATURED BANTER.
IS *THAT* ALL I'M GOOD FOR?!
U ...

"You're honest, so I feel like I can talk to you."
You're honest, so I feel like I can talk to you.
YOU AREN'T TALKING! YOU'RE WRITING!

YOUR SHORT STATURE AND FIERY NATURE ARE CUTE.
CUTE?!

ACTUALLY, MORE OF YOUR BANTER COULD'VE HELPED WHEN WE ROLLED THE DIE.
THAT'S RIGHT.
"I agree."
YEAH...IT WOULD'VE ?
THAT AGAIN?!

I BET NAJIMI BROUGHT US HERE TO MAKE FRIENDS...
...SO I DON'T CARE IF YOU'RE A BIT FEISTY.
!
AFTER ALL, ANCHI, YOU DIDN'T TRY TO LEAVE.
WHICH IS CHARMING.
STOP MAKING ME SOUND *CUDDLY*!!

"The way you push people away reminds me of someone else."
WHO? ISAGI? REI?
YEAH, ME TOO...
IT PROBABLY STEMS FROM INSECURITY.
ENOUGH! CONVER-SATION OVER!

THEY SAY THE OPPOSITE OF AFFECTION IS INDIFFERENCE, BUT ACTUAL ANTIPATHY LEADS TO FONDNESS. ANCHI ISN'T GOOD AT EXPRESSING HERSELF, BUT SHE IS FULL OF WARMTH.
HUH? UM, OKAY.
YEAH. YEAH? Y-YEAH.
NOD
?
URGH ...

Y-YOU...

...IDIOTS!

Not used to finding acceptance

HER INSULTS ARE GETTING SIMPLER!!

UM, DID NAJIMI ASK ANY OF YOU TO BRING SOMETHING?
!

YES! SOMETHING FUN, INTERESTING, OR TASTY!
Yay! Peace!
Peace!
RIGHT! DID YOU BRING SOMETHING, ANCHI?
!

CHINSUKO COOKIES.
OKINAWAN CHINSUKO
CHIN-SUKO!

IS THAT A PROBLEM?! I JUST WENT TO OKINAWA, OKAY?!
OKAY... WHAT ABOUT YOU, KOMI?
!

START TOMORROW!
100 CONVERSATION TOPICS
~NEVER FEEL AWKWARD AGAIN!~
COMMUNICATION IS A MUST!
READ IT IN 10 MINUTES!
MM-HMM...

FIRST, YOU NEED TO BE ABLE TO TALK.
!!
HOW ABOUT YOU, TSUZURA-FUJI?

SORRY.
OKINAWAN FAMOUS
CHINKUDO'S CHINSUKO
MORE CHINSUKO COOKIES ?!

YOU TOO?! WHY DO YOU HAVE THAT?!
S-SORRY! MY UNCLE JUST WENT TO OKINAWA!
UM... HOW ABOUT YOU, KOGOEN ?

SKWAWK
I BROUGHT A MEGAPHONE.
AND I STILL CAN'T HEAR YOU!!

I DOUBT IT WOULD'VE HELPED, BUT WHY DIDN'T YOU USE THAT BEFORE?!
SKWAWK
I THOUGHT IT MIGHT BE RUDE.
THE SQUAWKING IS LOUDER THAN YOU!

...
CHINSUKO
CHIN-SUKO AGAIN?!!

THREE OF US?! IS THAT EVEN POSSIBLE?! BUT NO ONE BROUGHT ANYTHING TO DRINK? WE'LL BE PARCHED!
SORRY. AN EMPLOYEE AT THE PET SHOP MY MOTHER'S FRIEND GOES TO JUST GOT BACK FROM—
I DON'T CARE HOW YOU GOT IT!

I LIKE SWEETS, BUT...
...I PREFER DORAYAKI.
IS THAT RELEVANT NOW?!
YOU DIDN'T *BRING* ANY, DID YOU?!

!
!
CRNCH CRNCH
CRNCH CRNCH
SHE'S EATING IT!
DOES IT TASTE GOOD?!
IT DOES? GOOD!

CRNCH CRNCH CRNCH CRNCH CRNCH CRNCH CRNCH CRNCH CRNCH
T
ANCHI, YOUR BANTER *KOFF* REALLY DOES LIVEN THE MOOD.
SKWAWK
IT INTRODUCES *KOFF* VARIETY.
YES *KOFF* IT DOES.
...!
K
NOW YOU'RE ALL *PARCHED!*

THREE OF US BROUGHT CHINSUKO AND THE OTHER TWO DIDN'T BRING ANYTHING WORTH MENTIONING!!
THAT'S WHY *YOU DON'T HAVE ANY FRIENDS!*

GASP!

AH HA HA!
THAT'S SO TRUE!

...
ARGH...

Communication 253 — The End

TOGYATTHER
I'm 30 and I've never had a girlfriend. Help!
TOGYATTHER
Apologize at your ancestors' grave.
TOGYATTHER
Shucks! You meanie, you! ♥
TOGYATTHER
Now I know why you're single.
TOGYATTHER
How's this design?
TOGYATTHER
It's boring. Spice it up.
TOGYATTHER
Thanks for dragging me, sinrabansyo-anti4404! ♥
TOGYATTHER
You're happy about that?! Dimwit!
ANTI
Her insults earned her minor fame.

Komi Can't Communicate

Komi Can't Communicate

Communication 254: Fantasies, Part 4

Who would you date?
-Anchi-

IT MAY BE THE WEEKEND, BUT YOU'RE TOO RELAXED!!
G
ANCHI ALREADY ?!

HEY, ARISA.
HOW'D YOUR ROOM GET SO DIRTY SO FAST?!
THERE'S UNDERWEAR EVERY-WHERE! WERE YOU *MOLD* IN A PREVIOUS LIFE?!
THIS PLACE IS FILTHY!
AND SMELLY!
SO *DIE!*

...
DO YOU HATE ME NOW?
DJANEL

...

I DON'T HATE YOU.

WHY IS YOUR KOTATSU STILL OUT?!
B-BUT...
... CLEAN UP!

THEN SHE HELPS ME CLEAN MY ROOM.
Heh heh...
NICE... THE DEMANDING-WIFE TYPE.
I LOOK FORWARD TO HAVING A GIRLFRIEND IN COLLEGE.
IS THAT WHAT COLLEGE STUDENTS ARE LIKE?

*This scene was pure fantasy. Any relation to real persons or events is coincidental.

Who would you date?
-Suzurafuji-

SWIP

SONODA (MY BOY-FRIEND) IS WALKING WITH ANOTHER GIRL...
OH NO... IS HE CHEATING ON ME?!
SHOULD I CONFRONT HIM?! BUT WHAT WOULD I SAY?!

I TOTALLY UNDER-STAND... I'M PLAIN LOOK-ING...
...AND BORING ...
...SO HE GOT TIRED OF ME.
HE DESERVES SOME-BODY CUTER ...
HM? SAKI?

UH... WHAH?!
WHAT'RE YOU DOING HERE?
OOPS. HAVEN'T YOU TWO MET?
KYAAH
I'M HIS LITTLE SISTER, RIBON! ARE YOU HIS GIRL-FRIEND?
HM?

I'M...
...SO RELIEVED!

Sis
"WOO-HOO! BRO'S IN LOVE!"
Bro
"SHUT UP AND SCRAM, SIS!"
THAT WAS OUR FIRST FANTASY FROM A GIRL'S POINT OF VIEW! B MADE SAKI CUTE THROUGH HER TEARS AND EVEN PORTRAYED HIS SISTER! ISN'T HE A GENIUS, G?!
UM... SURE.
*This scene was pure fantasy. Any relation to real persons or events is coincidental.

Who would you date?
-Kogoen-
RAAAH
RAAAH
MOSO
MOSO
MOSO
MOSO
SO
MOSO

RAAAH
RAAAH
IT'S TOO HOT TO BE OUT HERE CHEERING!
!
BAM
BAM

RAAAH
RAAAH
BAM
BAM BAM BAM
LET'S GO SOMEPLACE ALONE.
HUH? I CAN'T HEAR YOU OVER THE CHEERING!
RAAAH
RAAAH
BAM
BAM

Communication 254 — The End

Bonus Communication — The End

Komi Can't Communicate

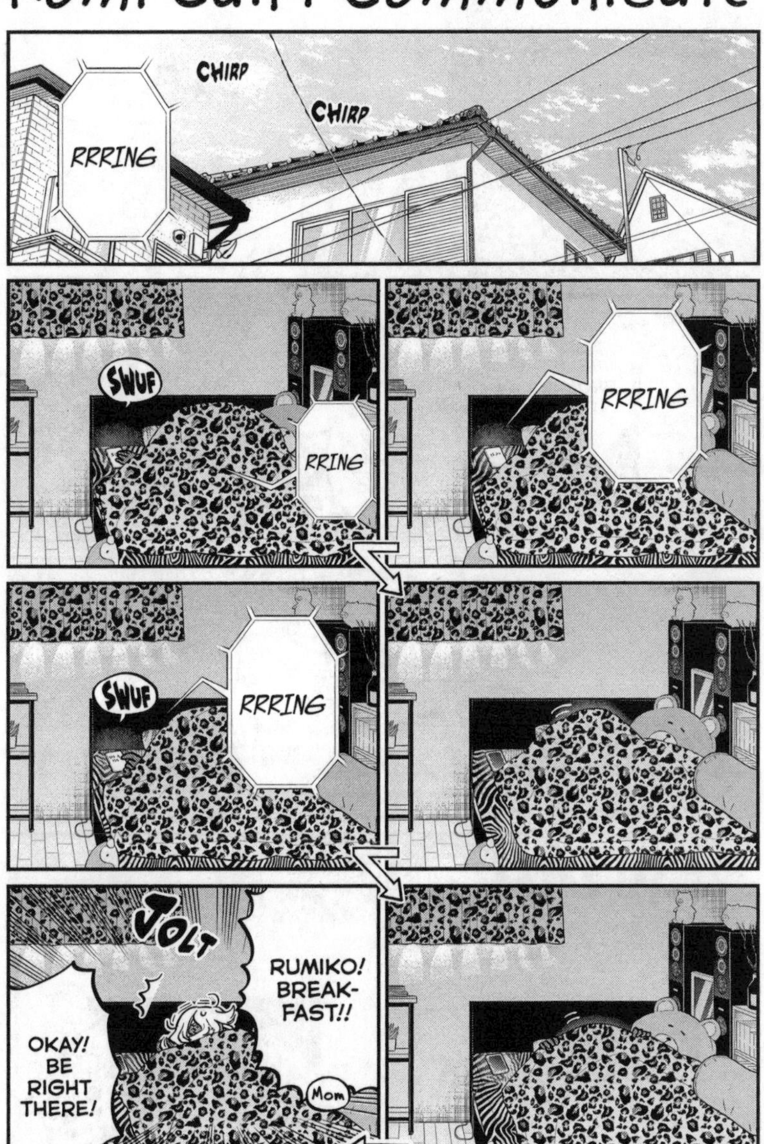

Communication 255: Hand Warmers

IT'S COLD!!
HWUF
She's trying to blame her phone.
IS MY PHONE BROKEN?
IT'S ALREADY PAST SEVEN?
DID MY ALARM GO OFF?
!
07:12
HWAP
AGH!
...

I'M LEAVING FOR SCHOOL!
WHOA! IT'S FREEZING OUT!

GOOD MORNING, MA'AM!
Good morning!
Have a good day!

!

GOOD MORNING, SHOKO!
TOU
UCH
?!!

!
AH HA HA! MY HANDS ARE WARM BECAUSE I WAS HOLDING HAND WARMERS!

I'VE GOT 'EM ALL OVER! LIKE TWO ON MY BACK!
They stick on!
PWAH
PWAH
!

GOOD MORNING, YOU TWO!
IT'S SURE GOTTEN COLDER!
!

HYAH!
FLINCH
!!
AH HA HA! DID YOU EXPECT COLD HANDS?
ACTUALLY, YOUR *CHEEKS* ARE COLD!
BUT MY HANDS ARE WARM!
UH...
...YEAH.

...!
Finally noticing her boldness
...
SH...
BWAAAAAAK
SHOKO, YOU SHOULD TOUCH HIS CHEEKS TOO!!
?!

BW
K
AAA
?!
MY CHEEKS ?!
T
THEY'RE... LIKE... TOTALLY AWESOME!!
AAK

...
...

KYAH
TCH

PWOOOOOOOO
W-WHAT'S WITH THEM?!
T

THE OTHER DAY, TADANO AND I GOT TRAPPED IN THE P.E. STORAGE ROOM.
HWAH?
?!
See communication 246.

SO...YOU SHOULD DO THAT TOO, RUMIKO.
T
WHAT? WHY?!

UM...

...I'M ALL FOR IT!
GNUP
T
SHE IS?!

After school

P.E. storage room

YOU TWO WERE TRAPPED IN HERE?
YES.
"Should I lock the door?"
N-NO! LEAVE IT OPEN!

ACTUALLY, YOU SHOULD COME WITH!
?!

WHAT'S THE POINT OF THIS?!
Nobody knew anymore.

IT'S KINDA CHILLY.
UH, YEAH.
WANT TO BORROW MY JACKET?
UM...NO THANKS! I'M FINE! I'VE GOT HAND WARMERS!

ARE YOU ALL RIGHT TOO, KOMI?
!!
NOD NOD

HERE. I'LL SHARE MY HAND WARMERS.
THEY'RE STILL WARM.
OH, THANKS.
!
...
YOU WERE IN HERE ALONE, HUH?
DID ANYTHING WEIRD HAPPEN?
N-NO, WE JUST TALKED!
I CAN'T TELL HER WHAT WE DID!

SO...
... WHAT'D YOU TALK ABOUT?
MOSTLY ABOUT ESCAPING OTORI'S HOUSE.
OH, THAT?

WE ALSO TALKED ABOUT YOU, MANBAGI.
!!
ME?
KOMI ASKED WHAT I THINK OF YOU.
SHE WHAT?!
!!

Y-YOU D-DID ?!
NOD
NOD
!!
!!
T
MAYBE I SHOULDN'T HAVE MENTIONED THAT?

AWKWARD SILENCE
OKAY, SO, UM...
... WHAT DID YOU SAY?

I SAID...

...I THINK OF YOU AS A FRIEND.

YOU THINK I'M A FRIEND, SO...

...I SHOULD BE HAPPY, RIGHT?

WE MET THROUGH KOMI, SO I GUESS...
...I'M THE FRIEND OF A FRIEND!
!

THAT'S JUST HOW HE TALKS, RIGHT? HE'S ALWAYS POLITE AROUND GIRLS!
HE ONLY LOOSENS UP AROUND BOYS! OR NAJIMI!
RIGHT ?!
!
NOD
OH, REALLY ?

WELL, IF WE'RE FRIENDS ...
...THEN BE MORE CASUAL WITH ME.

!

ALL RIGHT...

...I'LL DO THAT.

Gesture: "Wasn't that crazy-awesome?!"
FLUSTER
!!
Jeal-ous
T
?
Gesture: "Sorry for hogging him!"
FLUSTER
SHAKE SHAKE
!!
T
WHAT ARE YOU DOING?
YOU'RE TURNING RED. ARE YOU OKAY?
FWIP
!!!

Communication 255 — The End

Komi Can't Communicate

Komi Can't Communicate

UNIVERSITY ENTRANCE EXAM PATTERNS

Communication 256: Four-Way Talks

Komi Can't Communicate

WEAR THESE, TADANO.
HUH?

FIRST, WE'LL DISCUSS PRIVATE INFOR-MATION SUCH AS GRADES.
Head-phones
Eye mask
THEN WHY AM I EVEN HERE?!

ALL RIGHT, LET'S BEGIN.
WHAT A SCENE THIS MUST BE!

YOUR DAUGHTER'S GRADES ...
...ARE GOOD ENOUGH FOR A NATIONAL UNIVERSITY.
FOR EXAMPLE...

LET'S TAKE THOSE OFF NOW.
!

Humidity: 80 percent
DO YOU HAVE ANY QUESTIONS, MRS. ASE?
YES, MAY I?
GO AHEAD.

WHAT IS SHIBUKI LIKE AT SCHOOL?
SHE CAN BE SO TIMID. I WORRY.
!

UM, ME?

WHAT'S SHE LIKE AT SCHOOL? WELL...
...COMPARED TO THE PREVIOUS SEMESTER, SHE'S MORE OUTGOING.

ASE HAS ALWAYS BEEN SUPPORTIVE OF HER PEERS...
...AND SHE TOOK A LEADING ROLE BEHIND THE SCENES AT THE CULTURE FESTIVAL...
...THEREBY DEMON-STRATING PERSONAL GROWTH.

...

2－1
NEXT.

PARDON US.
ISAGI'S FATHER CAME?
Isagi's Father
Kiyoshi Isagi

PLEASE, HAVE A-
DFWSH
DFWSH
SQUEAK
WIPE WIPE
THEY'RE BOTH GERMA-PHOBES!

WE'LL RETURN AFTER WASHING OUR HANDS.
OH... OKAY.

ISAGI, YOU CAN AIM A LITTLE HIGHER.
ANYWAY, THE BOY MAY LISTEN NOW.

TAP
I HEARD YOU WERE INSTRUMENTAL IN MY DAUGHTER'S STUDENT COUNCIL CAMPAIGN...
...SO I MUST EXPRESS MY GRATITUDE.
BOW
UM, IT WAS NOTHING.

I'M A LAWYER AND MY DAUGHTER WANTS TO BE ONE TOO.
DON'T YOU THINK SHE'S CUTE? WELL, DON'T YOU?
UM, YEAH...I GUESS.

WELL, TRY ANYTHING AND I'LL MAKE YOU SUFFER!
?!

UM, I WOULD NEVER DO THAT!
GRRR
AND SHE WOULDN'T DATE ANYONE LIKE THAT.

ISAGI HAS A STRONG MORAL CORE...
...SO EVERYONE LOOKS UP TO HER AS STUDENT COUNCIL PRESIDENT.
THE PREVIOUS PRESIDENT WAS *IDIOSYN-CRATIC...*

...AND ISAGI HAS SHOWN GREAT FLEXIBILITY IN CARRYING ON HER LEGACY...
...SO I BELIEVE SHE'LL MAKE A FINE LAWYER.

...

2–1
PINCH
?!

OH, KATAI IS NEXT?

MAKOTO WILL INHERIT THE FAMILY DOJO, WHICH IS OF THE UTMOST IMPORTANCE, SO IF HE IS GOING TO PURSUE HIGHER EDUCATION, I BELIEVE THE BEST SUBJECT WOULD BE PHYSICAL EDUCATION, BUT WHAT IS YOUR OPINION AS HIS TEACHER?
BWA
BWA
BWA
...
HELP ME OUT HERE, TADANO.
?!

HELLO AGAIN, MRS. KATAI.
BWA
BWA
BWA
OH! HELLO, TADANO! THANK YOU FOR BEING FRIENDS WITH MAKOTO!
...

WELL ...
...KATAI IS GOOD AT BOTH SPORTS AND STUDY, SO A PHYSICAL EDUCATION DEGREE WOULD BE PERFECT.
!

HOWEVER, HE'S ALSO SENSITIVE AND KIND-HEARTED...
...AND CONFLICT AVERSE.

HE'S CAPABLE IN MANY AREAS AND HAS HIS OWN AMBITIONS, SO IT MIGHT BE WISE...
...TO TAKE TIME TO CONSIDER HIS OPTIONS.

...

2-1
RUMI ALWAYS USED TO SAY SHE WANTED TO BE A BRIDE!
HEY!
NOW IT'S A *COSMETIST* OR SOMETHING!
IT'S CALLED A *MAKE-UP ARTIST!*
BUT SHE DOESN'T HAVE ANY ARTISTIC SENSE, DOES SHE?
SHUT UP, MOM!
Mother Rukako
IN MY OPINION, SHE DOES.
REALLY?!
HER *GYARU* MAKEUP SURPRISED ME AT FIRST, BUT SHE ISN'T WEARING AS MUCH NOW, WHICH MAKES FOR A MORE NATURAL LOOK.
SHE WILL DEVELOP AESTHETIC SOPHISTICATION ALONG WITH OTHER SENSIBILITIES, SO THERE'S NO NEED TO WORRY.
HER DISTINCT TASTE WILL SERVE HER WELL IN THE FUTURE.
...

2-1
KYAH! HELLO, TADANO! IT'S BEEN A WHILE! COME VISIT AGAIN SOMETIME! IS YOUR MOTHER WELL?
HOW'S SHOKO DOING? OKAY, I HOPE?
Mother Shuko

WELL, KOMI'S A BIT DIFFICULT...
!!

SHE STOOD OUT FROM HER CLASSMATES FOR A WHILE, BUT, UM... I MEAN IN A GOOD WAY! A GOOD WAY!!
NOW SHE'S A FULLY INTEGRATED MEMBER OF THE CLASS.
SOCIALIZING IS MORE IMPORTANT TO SOME THAN OTHERS...
...BUT I THINK IT'S A POSITIVE CHANGE.

...

UM... BECOMING PRIME MINISTER MIGHT BE AIMING TOO HIGH, BUT NARUSE IS INDEED CHARISMATIC.
I APPRECIATE HIS MORAL SUPPORT, AND I THINK HE HAS EXCELLENT LEADERSHIP ABILITIES.

KOMETANI IS GOOD AT ASSESSING SITUATIONS. I RESPECT HIS ABILITY TO STAY CALM AND TAKE CONSTRUCTIVE ACTION.
THUS, HE WOULD SERVE WELL IN THE ROLE OF CHIEF PRIEST AT THE FAMILY TEMPLE.

OHAI IS, UM... HONEST ABOUT HER INTERESTS, AND I LOVE HER IRREPRESSIBLE VIBRANCY.
SHE'S EASY FOR ANYONE TO TALK TO. SHE'S PLAYFUL AND GUTSY, SO SHE'S A PLEASURE TO BE AROUND.

TORO'S DESIRE TO STUDY LITERATURE MAKES SENSE. WHILE SHE DOESN'T TALK MUCH, WHAT SHE DOES SAY IS ALWAYS INSIGHTFUL.
SHE HAS A GRASP OF THE HUMAN HEART THAT I'D LOVE TO SEE EXPRESSED THROUGH WRITING.

YOUR FAMILY ISN'T BUD-DHIST?
ANYWAY, TOTOI IS THE CLASS MOOD-MAKER.
HE'S INTELLIGENT BUT PERHAPS DIRECTS HIS INTELLIGENCE INTO QUESTIONABLE OUTLETS. NONETHELESS, I LIKE THAT ABOUT HIM.

TAKARAZUKA IS HANDSOME AND HAS MANY TALENTS. SHE WILL PLAY AN IMPORTANT ROLE WHEREVER SHE GOES.
HOWEVER, SHE SHOULDN'T TRY TOO HARD TO SATISFY OTHERS' EXPEC-TATIONS.

FUKUSUKI'S DESIRE TO BE A FASHION DESIGNER ISN'T MISPLACED. HE WAS EXTREMELY HELPFUL DURING THE CULTURE FESTIVAL.
HE WORKS FAST AND HAS GREAT DESIGN SENSE.
FUSHIMA DISPLAYED AN OUTSTANDING GRASP OF STORY WHILE PROVIDING NARRATION AT THE CULTURE FESTIVAL.
SHE ALSO HAS VISUAL ARTISTIC SENSE, WHICH MADE HER INDISPENSABLE BEHIND THE SCENES.
SHE HAS A KIND HEART. SHE'S ALSO MISCHIEVOUS, BUT IN A CHARMING WAY.
FUWA ALWAYS LIFTS YOUR SPIRITS.
BODO IS TOLERANT AND DEPENDABLE.
ODOKA REALLY CREEPS UP BEHIND YOU.

WHOA...
Upon receiving Tadano's praise, everyone went "Whoa..."

HITOHITO IS ALWAYS SURROUNDED BY A MATCHLESS BEAUTY, A GYARU WITH A DARK TAN, AND A MUSCLE-BOUND DUDE...

...AND HE WENT TO A SINGLES MEETUP DRESSED AS A GIRL.

HITO–

STOP TALK-ING!

Communication 256 — The End

NAJIMI IS JOKING, RIGHT?
Mom
WELL...
...UM ...
... ACTUALLY, IT'S TRUE.
But Najimi's exagger-ating...
IT'S TRUE?!
Mom

Komi Can't Communicate

Komi Can't Communicate

Communication 257: Sleepover Study Session

Komi Can't Communicate

!
Baked sweets
Cake

RUSTLE
Antibacterial wipes x 10
...

HMPH HMPH
First time visiting

!
STAAAARE

STAAARE

ONCE MORE
SNUF
SNUF
T M A
?!
ALCOHOL 50

SWIPE

K M A
...!!
STAAAARE

Isagi recleaned an already-clean room.

RUSTLE
Her own cushion (vacuum packed)
!

FWUF
Her own cush-ion
?!
SOAK

!
Studying

NO.

NO.
CALPAS WATER

NO.

Study Sessions
Nobody wants to study.
?!
PLIP
PLIP

...

!

Thirty minutes later
SKRK
SKRK
?!

Study begins.
1:00 PM

2:00 PM

3:00 PM

4:30 PM

18:00

!
NIGHTFALL

?
?
?
AWWW!
MOOD DOWN

!
NO... MOOD UP

ECO

HWUP
HWUP
It was cold out-side.
PWAH

?!

BVVVT
BVVVT

KACHAK

SWUP

CHAK
!

BYE
VROOM

Her own bed-ding
FWUF
?!

STAGGER
STAGGER

CLAP
CLAP

HEE
HEEE
BAM
BAM
BAM

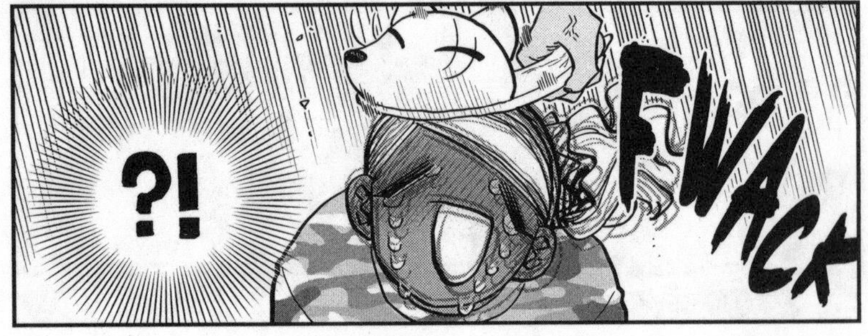
FWACK
?!

Rumiko's mom

WILT
Sleepovers
Moms get angry about noise.

Communication 257 — The End

Komi Can't Communicate

Before winter break

The test season ended...

...and everyone was starting to feel giddy.

2-1

Communication 258: Contact Info

The class is full of distinct personalities, but they generally get along well.
None-theless, there is a clear hierarchy!

Some students knew Komi's contact info...

...and some didn't!

Know!

Osana
Manbagi
Katai
Kometani
Isagi
Toro
Tadano
Naruse
Ase
Takarazuka

Don't Know!

Gekidan
Fukusuki
Bodo
Tsunde
Baba
Ninomai
Doji
Ohai
Inui
Fuwa
Odoka
Kicho
Santori
Ashitano
Totoi
Sarutahiko
Fushima
Urana
Ichinose
Shishima
Hafuri

No one lets it show, but they're insanely jealous of their classmates who know the angelic Komi's contact info.

Look!! I'll email this to you!!

GRNNND

They're all on amiable terms, but asking at this point would be embar-rassing.
2-1
But it's winter!

Which means they may only be Komi's classmate for another three months...
...so their panic inspired them into action!

Let the mission to get Komi's contact info...
...be-gin!!

SHALL I TELL YOU HER INFO? AND HER YOURS?
BLOOOOOM
NO, WE HAVE TO DO IT OUR-SELVES!!
They have to do it them-selves.

I'LL ASK FIRST.
Inui
HUNH? NO, I WILL!
Sarutahiko
HUNH?!

Inui and Sarutahiko don't get along.
HUNH?
HUNH?
HUNH?
HUNH?

SHUVVVVVVVVVVVVVV
HEY, UH, KOMI?!
?!

HE WANTS TO ASK YOU SOME-THIN'!!
?!
Sarutahiko chickened out.

...!
GRAH
GRAH
...!
...
?

SIIIGH...

UM... NEVER MIND.
?!
Inui chickened out.

SHUVVVVVV
WHY'D YOU PUSH IT OFF ON ME?!
CUZ YOU SAID YOU'D DO IT FIRST!!
THEN WHY FOLLOW ME, MORON?!
YOU'RE THE MORON!
WHY'D THEY EVEN BOTHER?!

I'M NEXT!
Bodo
Dat's right!!

UH... HI, KOMI.
!
UM... UM...

W- WANT A TANGER- INE?!
?!
Bodo chickened out.

THE WHITE PART IS GOOD FOR YOU!!
Bodo is motherly.
WHO IS THAT?!
WHO IS THAT?!

I'M NEXT!
Fuwa
Dat's right!!

...
...
L-LOOK, KOMI! MY STOMACH IS BOUNCY!! GIVE IT A TOUCH!
POINNNG
?!
Fuwa chick-ened out.

!
!
POING POING
Fuwa is bouncy.
Jealous of physical contact between Fuwa and Komi

I WAS UP ALL NIGHT DECIDING HOW TO APPROACH HER.
Fushima

AND I DECIDED TO *RAP.*
?!

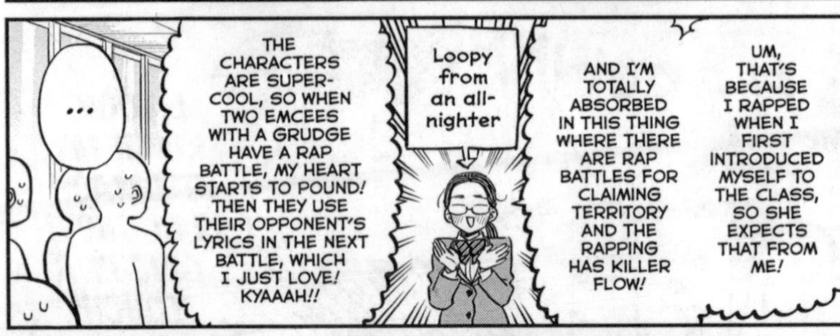
UM, THAT'S BECAUSE I RAPPED WHEN I FIRST INTRODUCED MYSELF TO THE CLASS, SO SHE EXPECTS THAT FROM ME!
AND I'M TOTALLY ABSORBED IN THIS THING WHERE THERE ARE RAP BATTLES FOR CLAIMING TERRITORY AND THE RAPPING HAS KILLER FLOW!
Loopy from an all-nighter
THE CHARACTERS ARE SUPER-COOL, SO WHEN TWO EMCEES WITH A GRUDGE HAVE A RAP BATTLE, MY HEART STARTS TO POUND! THEN THEY USE THEIR OPPONENT'S LYRICS IN THE NEXT BATTLE, WHICH I JUST LOVE! KYAAAH!!
...

YOU'LL WANT TO DIE AGAIN, SO DON'T.
Dat's right!
!!
*See vol. 10, page 29 for Fushima's rapping.

LEAVE THIS TO ME!
Ohai
OHAI ?!

GIMME YOUR CONTACT INFO... GIMME YOUR CONTACT INFO...
KOMI!
!!

GIMME YOUR CONTACT INFO... GIMME YOUR CONTACT INFO...
GIMME YOUR...

WHAT SHAPE ARE YOUR BOOBS?
GAH! I COULDN'T HELP IT!!
Ohai likes boobs. ♥
A、Round
B、Swooping
C、conical
All
GYA AAA AAH!

I'M NEXT!
Totoi
NO! NOT RIGHT AFTER OHAI!
IT'D BE PERVE OVER-LOAD!
WE CAN'T LET HIM CHAT UP KOMI!
Dat's right!
Totoi isn't that holy.
HERE I GO...
Fukusuki
NOT YOU EITHER!
Dat's right!!
Fukusuki likes sexy clothes.
LET US HANDLE THIS!
Santori
Shishima
Ichinose
Ninomai
IT'S THE NUMBER GUYS!
SWOOSH
...
All four chick-ened out.
THEY DIDN'T EVEN SPEAK!
THEN WHY EVEN SHOW UP?!
Dat's right!!
The number guys just make up numbers.

I HAVE DEVISED THE PERFECT PLAN.
Kicho
EXCEL-LENT!

Kicho left a magnifying glass on Komi's desk with a grain of rice engraved with his contact information...
TEL
193 1811-8999
MAIL
kichou.
men10529
@yahho.ne.jp
...assuming that Komi would wonder what was written on the rice and pick up the magnifying glass to inspect it, leading to her sending an email out of curiosity...
...and thereby completing the exchange of information in the most natural of ways.
WHAT?!
Kicho is highly organized.

Coming in for class

!

GLANCE
GLANCE
!
?
?

Taking the magnifying glass to lost and found.

Replay
Rice upon which Kicho painstakingly inscribed his contact info
Breeze

I DON'T NEED YOUR CONTACT INFO ANYWAY!!
Tsunde
Tsunde is tsundere.
?!

Komi...
Mwa ha...
Odoka
?!
Odoka likes to scare people.

I...I CAN DO THIS!
Doji (new character)
DOJI?!

WHOOPS!
TRIP
Phone
DOJI!!
Doji is clumsy.

YOU'RE ALL SO HELPLESS! SO I'LL HANDLE THIS!
Dat's right!
Ashitano (new character)
ASHITANO ?!

WOULD YOU LIKE TO EXCHANGE CONTACT INFOR-MATION?
!
All
WHOA!! SHE DID IT!

FUMP
?

She got burnt out and turned white.
Asking the question took all she had.
Jo Ashitano burns out.
?!

Urana sells fortunes.
YOUR LUCKY ITEM TODAY IS SOMETHING WITH CONTACT INFORMATION WRITTEN ON IT!
AND IT'S EVEN LUCKIER IF YOU BUY IT FROM A SAGITTARIAN STUDENT FORTUNE-TELLER WITH BLOOD TYPE AB! ONLY $3 FOR A LIMITED TIME!
?!
Urana
Hafuri is bubbly.
KOMI! LET'S EXCHANGE BEEPER INFO!!
YOU'D LOOK SO CUTE WITH ONE-LENGTH HAIR!
Dat's right!!
?!
Hafuri (new character)
OH, GIVE TO M-E-E-E YOUR PRIVATE NUMBERRR!
SHOW M-E-E-E YOUR PHONE!
Can't understand because Gekidan is singing
?
Gekidan
Clapping anyway
CLAPCLAPCLAP
Gekidan is dramatic.
GIVE IT A TRY, BABA!
CAN'T DO DAT.
She didn't say "Dat's right!"
Baba
Baba is a big follower.

Every-
one
failed.

WE SUCK AT THIS...
WINTER BREAK WILL BE MISER-ABLE...
LET'S GET OUTTA HERE ...
SHUFL
SHUFL

!

TATMP

!

Huh?
No way...

Almost crying because everyone is staring
TREMMBLE
?!

Y...

YOUR CONTACT...

...INFO ...

...

She wanted to ask them too.

Communication 258 — The End

Komi Can't Communicate

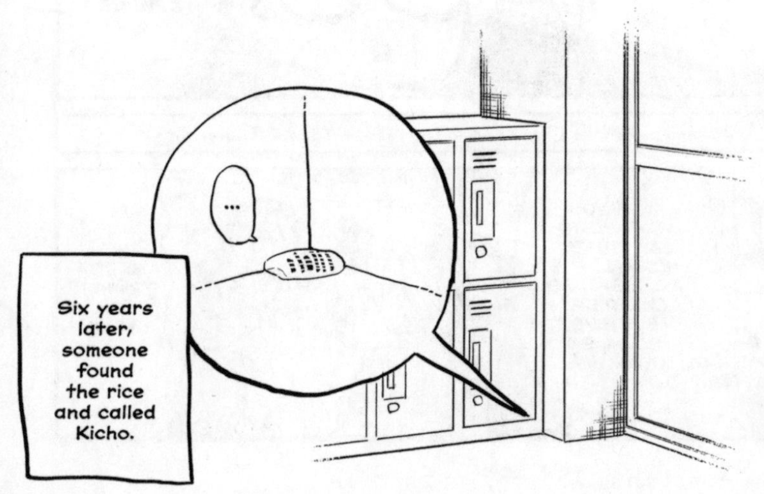
...
Six years later, someone found the rice and called Kicho.

Komi Can't Communicate Bonus

Tadano's Future

Can Komi Make 100 Friends? The Higashi-Sagami Triumvirate

Komi Can't Communicate Bonus

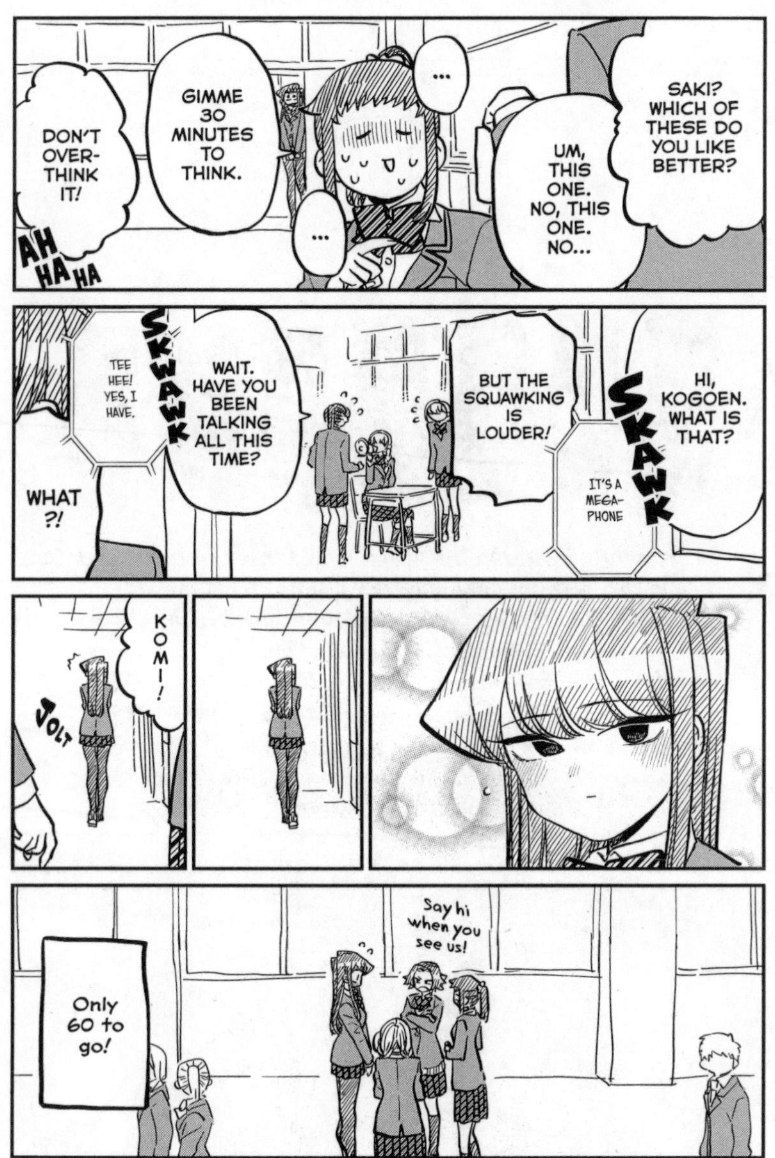

Tomohito Oda won the grand prize for *World Worst One* in the 70th Shogakukan New Comic Artist Awards in 2012. Oda's series *Digicon*, about a tough high school girl who finds herself in control of an alien with plans for world domination, ran from 2014 to 2015. In 2015, *Komi Can't Communicate* debuted as a one-shot in *Weekly Shonen Sunday* and was picked up as a full series by the same magazine in 2016.

Komi Can't Communicate

VOL. 19
Shonen Sunday Edition

Story and Art by Tomohito Oda

English Translation & Adaptation/John Werry
Touch-Up Art & Lettering/Eve Grandt
Design/Julian [JR] Robinson
Editor/Pancha Diaz

COMI-SAN WA, COMYUSHO DESU. Vol. 19
by Tomohito ODA

Original Japanese edition published by SHOGAKUKAN.
English translation rights in the United States of America, Canada, the United Kingdom, Ireland, Australia and New Zealand arranged with SHOGAKUKAN.

Original Cover Design/Masato ISHIZAWA + Bay Bridge Studio

Printed in the U.S.A.

Published by VIZ Media, LLC
P.O. Box 77010
San Francisco, CA 94107

10 9 8 7 6 5 4 3 2 1
First printing, June 2022

viz.com

shonensunday.com

PARENTAL ADVISORY
KOMI CAN'T COMMUNICATE is rated T for Teen and is recommended for ages 13 and up.

This is the last page!

Komi Can't Communicate has been printed in the original Japanese format to preserve the orientation of the artwork.

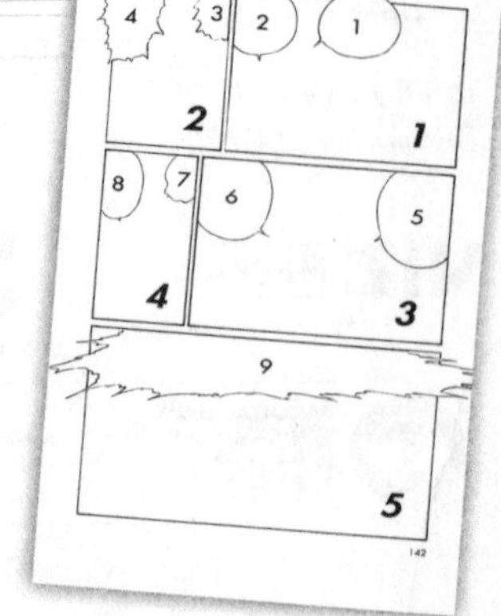

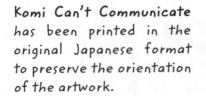

Follow the action this way.